SandCastle 3

Vowel Blends

ou

Mary Elizabeth Salzmann

Published by SandCastle™, an imprint of ABDO Publishing Company, 4940 Viking Drive, Edina, Minnesota 55435.

Printed in the United States.

Cover and interior photo credits: Comstock, Digital Stock, Eyewire Images, PhotoDisc, Stockbyte

Library of Congress Cataloging-in-Publication Data

Salzmann, Mary Elizabeth, 1968-
  Ou / Mary Elizabeth Salzmann.
    p. cm. -- (Vowel blends)
  ISBN 1-57765-458-7
  1. Readers (Primary) [1. Readers.] I. Title.

  PE1119 .S2342415 2001
  428.1--dc21

                                                                    00-056568

The SandCastle concept, content, and reading method have been reviewed and approved by a national advisory board including literacy specialists, librarians, elementary school teachers, early childhood education professionals, and parents.

Let Us Know

After reading the book, SandCastle would like you to tell us your stories about reading. What is your favorite page? Was there something hard that you needed help with? Share the ups and downs of learning to read. We want to hear from you! To get posted on the ABDO Publishing Company Web site, send us email at:

sandcastle@abdopub.com

About SandCastle™
Nonfiction books for the beginning reader

- Basic concepts of phonics are incorporated with integrated language methods of reading instruction. Most words are short, and phrases, letter sounds, and word sounds are repeated.

- Readability is determined by the number of words in each sentence, the number of characters in each word, and word lists based on curriculum frameworks.

- Full-color photography reinforces word meanings and concepts.

- "Words I Can Read" list at the end of each book teaches basic elements of grammar, helps the reader recognize the words in the text, and builds vocabulary.

- Reading levels are indicated by the number of flags on the castle.

Look for more SandCastle books in these three reading levels:

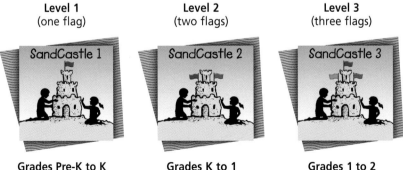

Level 1 (one flag)	**Level 2** (two flags)	**Level 3** (three flags)
Grades Pre-K to K 5 or fewer words per page	**Grades K to 1** 5 to 10 words per page	**Grades 1 to 2** 10 to 15 words per page

Courtney has fun with her dollhouse.

She plays for many hours.

ou

Kourtney gets a drink
from the fountain.

Then she will wipe
her mouth.

7

Young-Soo and his sister
are at the playground.

They ride the
merry-go-round.

Souzan and her cousin
lounge on the beach on
a sunny day.

ou

Emmylou and Jourdan use the mouse to work on the computer.

These four friends play touch football in the front yard.

Doug pitches from
the mound.

He tries to get the
batter out.

17

Douglas and Louis are on a campout.

They like to sleep in their tent.

ou

What are Dougal and his grandma building out of wood?

(birdhouse)

Words I Can Read

Nouns

A noun is a person, place, or thing

batter (BAT-ur) p. 17

beach (BEECH) p. 11

birdhouse (BURD-houss) p. 21

campout (KAM-pout) p. 19

computer (kuhm-PYOO-tur) p. 13

cousin (KUHZ-uhn) p. 11

day (DAY) p. 11

dollhouse (DOL-houss) p. 5

drink (DRINGK) p. 7

fountain (FOUN-tuhn) p. 7

friends (FRENDZ) p. 15

fun (FUHN) p. 5

grandma (GRAND-ma) p. 21

hours (OURZ) p. 5

merry-go-round (MER-ee–goh–round) p. 9

mound (MOUND) p. 17

mouse (MOUSS) p. 13

mouth (MOUTH) p. 7

playground (PLAY-ground) p. 9

sister (SISS-tur) p. 9

tent (TENT) p. 19

touch football (TUHCH FUT-bal) p. 15

wood (WUD) p. 21

yard (YARD) p. 15

Proper Nouns

A proper noun is the name of a person, place, or thing

Courtney (KORT-nee) p. 5

Doug (DUG) p. 17

Dougal (DOO-guhl) p. 21

Douglas (DUG-luhss) p. 19

Emmylou (EM-ee-loo) p. 13

Jourdan (JOR-duhn) p. 13

Kourtney (KORT-nee) p. 7

Louis (LOO-iss) p. 19

Souzan (SOO-zuhn) p. 11

Young-Soo (yuhng–SOO) p. 9

Pronouns

A pronoun is a word that replaces a noun

he (HEE) p. 17   **they** (THAY) pp. 9, 19   **what** (WUHT) p. 21
she (SHEE) pp. 5, 7

Verbs

A verb is an action or being word

are (AR) pp. 9, 19, 21   **lounge** (LOUNJ) p. 11   **tries** (TRYEZ) p. 17
building (BIL-ding) p. 21   **pitches** (PICH-ez) p. 17   **use** (YOOZ) p. 13
get (GET) p. 17   **play** (PLAY) p. 15   **will** (WIL) p. 7
gets (GETSS) p. 7   **plays** (PLAYZ) p. 5   **wipe** (WIPE) p. 7
has (HAZ) p. 5   **ride** (RIDE) p. 9   **work** (WURK) p. 13
like (LIKE) p. 19   **sleep** (SLEEP) p. 19

Adjectives

An adjective describes something

four (FOR) p. 15   **his** (HIZ) pp. 9, 21   **their** (THAIR) p. 19
front (FRUHNT) p. 15   **many** (MEN-ee) p. 5   **these** (THEEZ) p. 15
her (HUR) pp. 5, 7, 11   **sunny** (SUH-nee) p. 11

Adverbs

An adverb tells how, when, or where
something happens

out (OUT) pp. 17   **then** (THEN) p. 7

Glossary

computer – A machine that can store, process, and retrieve information.

fountain – A stream or jet of water used for drinking or decoration.

mound – A raised area for the pitcher in the center of a baseball field.

playground – An outdoor area, often with swings, slides, and other equipment where children can play.

More ou Words

around	found	pouch
blouse	group	shout
count	house	trouble
doubt	loud	would
enough	our	your